To Joseph from Suzy

STERLING CHILDREN'S BOOKS
New York

An Imprint of Sterling Publishing Co., Inc.
1166 Avenue of the Americas
New York, NY 10036

ISBN 978-1-4549-3203-1

Distributed in Canada by Sterling Publishing Co., Inc.
c/o Canadian Manda Group, 664 Annette Street
Toronto, Ontario M6S 2C8, Canada
Distributed in the United Kingdom by GMC Distribution Services
Castle Place, 166 High Street, Lewes, East Sussex BN7 1XU, England
Distributed in Australia by NewSouth Books
45 Beach Street, Coogee, NSW 2034, Australia

For information about custom editions, special sales, and premium and corporate purchases, please contact Sterling Special Sales at 800-805-5489 or specialsales@sterlingpublishing.com.

Manufactured in China

Lot #:
2 4 6 8 10 9 7 5 3 1
10/18

sterlingpublishing.com

PHOTOGRAPHS: Getty Images: Blend Images: 3, 7; Corbis: 2 inset right; EHStock: 4 inset; Shoji Fujita/Digital Vision: 9, 10; Hulton Archive: 2 inset left; Erik Isakson/Tetra Images: 14; martinedoucet: 23; Ryan McVay:i
iStock: AndreyPopov: 4 inset top; Charles Mann: 5 left; RBFried: 11, 21; Andrew Rich: 17, back cover bottom; RonTech2000: 18; sandrak: 13; Aimin Tang: 2 inset right, 24; video1: cover; xjben: 20
Shutterstock: William Hager: 6; David Lee: 1; pixelsnap: 2 and 4 background; tammykayphoto: back cover top
Thinkstock: George Doyle: 5; Cathy Yeulet: 19

LET'S PLAY

BASEBALL

*Everything You Need to Know
for Your First Practice*

by **Susan Blackaby**

STERLING CHILDREN'S BOOKS
New York

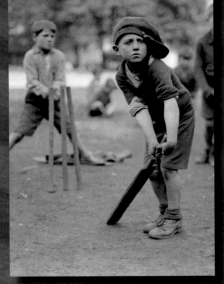

History

For hundreds of years, kids around the world have played games using sticks and balls. Kids in England played two stick-and-ball games. One was called rounders and one was cricket. When kids from England came to America, they brought their games with them. Little by little, baseball took shape. People formed baseball clubs and wrote a set of rules. Before long, baseball became America's pastime. Fans have been playing and watching baseball in the United States for almost 200 years!

GLOSSARY

Here are some baseball words to know. Watch for them as you read.

Bases—The four points of a baseball diamond (first base, second base, third base, and home plate); you stand at home plate to bat and must touch each base in the proper order to score a run.

Batter—The player who is up to hit.

Catcher—The player catching balls behind home plate.

Diamond—The infield, named for its shape: ◇.

Infield—The baseball diamond.

Inning—A part of the game during which each team gets a chance to bat while the other team plays defense.

Out—An action that stops the team at bat; each team at bat gets three outs per inning.

Outfield—Part of the field beyond the diamond and bordered by the first and third baselines.

Pitcher—The player who pitches the ball to the batter on the other team; your coach will most likely be the pitcher at your games.

Pitcher's mound—Where the pitcher stands in the middle of the infield.

Run—A point scored when a player rounds all the bases and returns to home plate.

Strike—When the batter takes a swing at a fair pitch and misses.

Tag—When the fielder touches the base while holding the ball or touches a runner while holding the ball.

Umpire—A person who enforces the rules during the game.

The Gear

To play baseball, you only need a few things: a bat, a ball, and a glove! Bats come in different sizes. Test them out to see which one feels the best. For now, you will use a ball that is a little bigger and softer than what big kids and pros use.

You will also need a glove. When you try one on, be sure you can open and close your hand. It will feel stiff! It will soften up as you keep playing with it. When you are not using your glove, keep a baseball in it so the glove keeps its shape.

When you play on a team, you might get a uniform. Matching shirts and caps make your teammates easy to spot. The **catcher** will get full gear, including a mask, a special glove, a chest protector, and shin guards. Batters get a protective helmet when they get up to hit.

BASEBALL BASICS

To play baseball, you need to learn how to bat, throw, and catch. Can you run? Good. That's one skill you already have down!

Batting

The first rule of batting is be careful! The only thing you want to hit is the ball! Pick up a bat when it is your turn to go up to the plate. Otherwise, leave bats alone.

GET SET TO SWING:

- Stand facing the plate with your feet apart and your knees bent.

- Turn your head toward the **pitcher**.

- Stay relaxed. Give your body a good shake if you feel tight. Shift your weight to the balls of your feet to keep loose.

- Get a grip. Lay the bat across your fingers and then wrap your hands around the handle. Keep your wrists loose and your knuckles lined up.

- Hold the bat above your shoulder. Point the big end to the sky.

- When the ball comes to you, plant your back foot and step into the swing with your front foot.

- Start the swing with your hips. Pull the bat all the way around to follow through.

Remember not to let go of the bat! A flying bat is a scary thing. If you get a hit, you can gently toss the bat to the ground as you run to first base.

You can bat left even if you throw right. Try batting both right and left. Go with the one that feels best. If you bat left, you have your left hand on top and the bat over your left shoulder. If you bat right, you have your right hand on top and the bat over your right shoulder.

Throwing

Throwing a baseball requires using the whole body.

THROWING TIPS:

- Grip the ball with your fingers across the seams. Keep your wrist, elbow, and shoulder loose, loose, loose.

- Rotate your shoulder as if you are giving a high five.

- Bend your elbow.

- Flick your wrist as you let go of the ball.

- Stand with your chest facing away from your catching partner. Use your glove to help you aim at your partner's heart. Don't take your eyes off your partner as you throw. Bring your elbow back and around. When the ball lines up with your partner, take a step forward and let go of the ball. Swing your arm around in front of your body to follow through.

- Start softly! Work on your aim. Practice with a pal as often as you can. Once you can hit your mark, then you can throw harder and move farther away from your partner.

Catching

Get ready for the ball to come your way. Stand with your feet apart and your knees bent. When you see where the ball is heading, move to catch it.

Your baseball glove helps you catch. It keeps your hand from getting smacked by the ball. The best way to break in a stiff new glove is to catch, catch, catch, catch!

To catch a ball that comes in high, hold your glove so your palm faces out. To catch a ball that comes in low, hold your glove so your palm faces up. Catch the ball in the pocket of your glove. Use your bare hand to trap the catch. You can practice on your own by tossing the ball high in the air and catching it.

You will hear people say, "Keep your eye on the ball." They mean watch the ball all the way into your glove. Even though watching the ball come right at you may be scary, keep your eyes open. If you don't watch the ball, it will be impossible to catch. If the sun gets in your eyes, try wearing a baseball cap or sunglasses.

THE FIELD

A baseball field is split into two parts—the **infield** and the **outfield**.

The infield is the baseball **diamond**. At each point there is a **base**. Home plate is at the bottom tip of the diamond. First base is on the right point. Second base is on the top point. Third base is on the left point. The **pitcher's mound** is in the middle.

The outfield is the area between the diamond and the fence. The first base line and the third base line mark its borders.

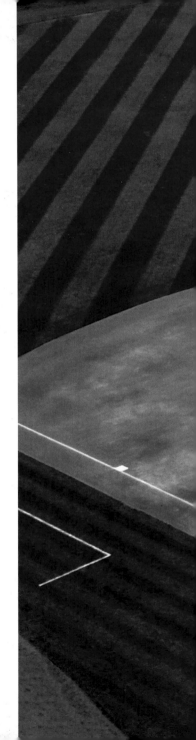

SHORTSTOP

SECOND BASE

THIRD BASE

PITCHER

BALL

CATCHER

Notice how the different position players
react to this infield hit.

FIRST BASE

THE PLAYERS

A baseball team is made up of infielders and outfielders. Infielders are the catcher and the pitcher; players at first, second, and third **base**; and a player in between second base and third base, called a shortstop. You may or may not have a shortstop on your team—it's a demanding defensive position, and can be dangerous until you get older and have more experience with the game. Outfielders play zones in right field, center field, and left field. Everyone on your team will learn to play all the positions. And everyone on the team takes a turn at bat.

When big kids and pros play, nine players are on the field. The pitcher pitches to batters. In your games, there may be more than nine players on the field, and the coach will pitch to you. The pitcher will stand on the mound, ready to step in and field balls that are hit.

HOW THE GAME IS PLAYED

A baseball game is split into parts called **innings**. Big kids and pros play nine innings. They score as much as they can. If there is a tie, they play more innings. You'll play for about an hour. Your games will have six innings or fewer.

During an inning, each team gets a chance to bat. A team keeps batting until it gets three outs. In some leagues, a team stops batting after it scores five runs.

At the top of the inning, the visiting team is at bat. The home team is on the field. At the bottom of the inning, the home team is at bat. When the home team gets three outs or five runs, the inning is over.

The Top of the Inning

The first half of an inning is called the top. Your team is up, and you are the batter! A few things might happen:

You might swing at the ball and miss it. That is called a **strike**. If you get three strikes, you are **out**.

You might hit the ball nice and high! But if a fielder catches the ball before it touches the ground, you will be out.

You might hit the ball and zip to first base. But you might not beat the **tag**. You will be out if a fielder holding the ball touches you or touches the base before you can get there.

Or . . . Pow! You get a hit!

You drop your bat and run to first base. No one tags you. You are safe!

Get ready to go, but stay on the base. You can't start running to the next base until a **batter** on your team hits the ball.

When the batter gets a hit, take off! You want to beat the fielder to the next base. Your coach will tell you if you can keep running. Touch a foot to each base as you go around. When you land back on home plate, your team gets a **run**! A run is worth one point.

The Bottom of the Inning

The second half of an inning is called the bottom. Your team is on the field. Some players are in the infield, and some players are in the outfield. Outfielders will spread out. They will stay loose with their feet apart and their knees bent. They will be ready to catch a batted ball that comes their way. Outfielders catch the ball and throw it to infielders.

Infielders stick close to the bases. If you are playing second base, you stand nearby. You are ready to catch any ball that comes your way from an outfielder.

Once you have the ball, hang onto it if you have a play. You can tag the runner between bases, or you can step on the base before the runner gets there. Either of those plays will count as an out. If you don't have a play, see if another infielder does. You can throw the ball to a teammate so that he or she can get an out. If you get the ball, but there is no play to make, and no play for your teammates to make, hang onto the ball or send it back to the pitcher.

DRILLS BUILD SKILLS!

Between games, you will practice with your team. Your coach will help you build up your strength and your speed. During practice, you will:

- Get lots of chances to hit baseballs.

- Learn how to place your hand and glove to catch the ball at any speed and any height.

- Learn the setup, launch, and follow-through of your throw so that you hit your mark every time.

- Run around the bases over and over again.

What do you need to do to learn to play and keep getting better? Pay attention, ask questions, and practice, practice, practice. And most important of all, *keep your eye on the ball*. All the time.

Game Day

Here are some Game Day tips:

- Make sure you are ready to go. If you are late for the lineup, you might not get to play. Stow your gear in a bag so that you can grab it and go. You don't want to be searching all over the place for your glove when it's time to leave.
- Arrive on time and ready to play.
- Listen for the call! The **umpire** will help you follow the rules. Coaches will make sure everyone gets time to play.
- Keep your mind on the action and your eye on the ball at *all times*. Even if you are on the bench in the dugout, watch the ball.
- Play hard and play fair. Goods sports make good players.
- Cheer for your teammates when you are on the bench or on the field.
- High fives all around! Praise the players and thank the coaches on BOTH teams.
- Thank the person who brings the snacks.

Baseball takes teamwork and speed. It is a great way to build skills and make lifelong friends. Pick up your glove and pick up a game. Play ball!

A Note to Your Biggest Fan

Parents and caregivers can play a key role in helping kids who are stepping up to the plate for the first time.

Model model behavior. Teamwork and sportsmanship are critical to any game. Provide encouragement and support to your child, to your child's team, and to your child's opponents. Show respect to the coaches and other volunteers on both teams.

Let the coach coach. You have a couple of jobs to do, but coaching isn't one of them. Be sure your child is on time and ready to play, then take a seat and take it easy.

Away from the field, ask the coach to provide practice tips that will support the team methods and message, and privately discuss any concerns you have about your child's playing time or performance.

Temper your temper. As any major leaguer will tell you, striking out, dropping an easy catch, and losing are all part of the game. Missteps and missed calls can be frustrating for everybody. Keep cool! The point of baseball at this level is for your child to develop new skills, get some fresh air, play with friends, and have fun. Learning to take mistakes in stride will help your child become a happier, more confident player.